ALBUCASIS

THE FATHER OF MODERN SURGERY

PHYSICIANS, SCIENTISTS, AND MATHEMATICIANS OF THE ISLAMIC WORLD™

ALBUCASIS

THE FATHER OF MODERN SURGERY

BRIDGET LIM
AND FRED RAMEN

ROSEN PUBLISHING®
New York

Published in 2017 by The Rosen Publishing Group, Inc.
29 East 21st Street, New York, NY 10010

First Edition

Library of Congress Cataloging-in-Publication Data

Names: Lim, Bridget, author. | Ramen, Fred, author.
Title: Albucasis (Abu al-Qasim al-Zahrawi) : the father of modern surgery / Bridget Lim and Fred Ramen.
Description: First edition. | New York : Rosen Publishing, 2017. | N2017 | Series: Physicians, scientists, and mathematicians of the Islamic world | | Includes bibliographical references and index.
Identifiers: LCCN 2015047181 | ISBN 9781508171409 (library bound)
Subjects: LCSH: Abau al-Qaasim Khalaf ibn Abbaas al-Zahraawai, -1013?--Juvenile literature. | Physicians--Arab countries--Biography--Juvenile literature. | Surgeons--Arab countries--Biography--Juvenile literature. | Physicians--Spain--Biography--Juvenile literature. | Surgeons--Spain--Biography--Juvenile literature. | Medicine, Arab--Spain--History--Juvenile literature. | Medicine, Medieval--Spain--Juvenile literature.
Classification: LCC R144.A2 R36 2017 | DDC 610.92--dc23
LC record available at http://lccn.loc.gov/2015047181

Manufactured in China

CONTENTS

INTRODUCTION 6

CHAPTER ONE
EARLY MEDITERRANEAN CIVILIZATIONS 8

CHAPTER TWO
THE ARAB CAPITAL OF CÓRDOBA 27

CHAPTER THREE
PHYSICIANS OF THE ANCIENT WORLD 46

CHAPTER FOUR
MEDICINE IN THE ISLAMIC WORLD 61

CHAPTER FIVE
ALBUCASIS'S ACHIEVEMENTS 74

CHAPTER SIX
THE END OF MUSLIM POWER IN AL-ANDALUS 86

GLOSSARY 99
FOR MORE INFORMATION 103
FOR FURTHER READING 106
BIBLIOGRAPHY 108
INDEX 109

INTRODUCTION

During the period known as the Dark Ages, the term traditionally used for the period between the fall of the Roman Empire in 476 CE and about 1000 CE, much of the impressive learning and advances that had taken place in the ancient world was lost and forgotten in Europe. At the time, Latin, the language of the Roman Empire, was known only to a few, mostly clergymen. Even rarer, at least outside the Byzantine Empire, was knowledge of Greek, which meant that the great works of philosophers such as Plato and Aristotle were unknown to most. Medicine was almost a lost art in Europe; disease killed many people before they turned twenty, and major surgery was almost always fatal.

Yet there were still parts of the world where the hoard of knowledge accumulated by the Greeks and Romans continued unabated, where works by Plato and Aristotle remained influential, where the study of medicine was a vital art, and where medical practitioners achieved a level of learning not seen in Europe until the end of the Renaissance, nearly five hundred years later. This was in Europe itself, just over the Pyrenees from France, on the Iberian Peninsula, a land called by its conquerors al-Andalus but that we know as

Spain. From this colony of learning would come the greatest physician of his age, Abu al-Qasim Khalaf ibn Abbas az-Zahrawi or Abu al-Qaṣim, known to the Latin speaking world as Albucasis.

Albucasis was born in 936 CE in the town of Medinat al-Zahra near Córdoba in al-Andalus, the Arabic name referring to parts of the Iberian Peninsula under Muslim rule. Al-Andalus (known to Westerners as Andalusia) was a region important in antiquity and that would later become the dynamo behind Europe's expansion and conquest of the Americas. At the time of Albucasis's birth, al-Andalus was the center of a flourishing culture that valued science and philosophy, where the two disciplines often complimented one another as traditional Islamic theology and law was embraced alongside the secular sciences of mathematics, physics, anatomy, biology, chemistry, and astronomy.

Among the many Islamic physicians and scientists who advanced medical science in their lifetimes, Albucasis would codify the art of surgery in an encyclopedic work that is still read today, *al-Tasrif*. His story is intimately connected to the history of Islam and how Muslims preserved the knowledge of the old Roman world, information that Europe would not rediscover for another four hundred years.

CHAPTER ONE

EARLY MEDITERRANEAN CIVILIZATIONS

Albucasis was a Muslim living in the most powerful Muslim region west of Baghdad (the chief city in the Muslim world and home to the successors of the prophet Muhammad). To understand how a region of Europe would be dominated by a non-European people for the better part of a millennium—and the effect that Islam and Arabic culture would have in shaping Europe's future, we must first go back and explore the history of the Mediterranean region, the crossroads of two continents and the basin of European civilization for more than five thousand years.

MESOPOTAMIA AND OTHER EARLY CIVILIZATIONS

Ever since the first empires of Mesopotamia extended themselves to the shores of the Mediterranean, the peoples living around this vast inland stretch of water have communicated, fought, and shared knowledge with one another in the process of forging the continent of Europe.

The first cities appeared in Mesopotamia in about 5000 BCE. Here, for the first time, agriculture made it possible for thousands of people to live close to each other. The goals and advancements of these new societies remain the basis of civilization throughout the world: writing, to preserve records; mathematics, to manage supplies; and codes of laws, to govern people. In time, the cities combined into the first kingdoms and then empires, warring against each other for control of the Fertile Crescent, the region between the Tigris and Euphrates Rivers.

Soon other cultures had founded their own civilizations. The first to border directly on the Mediterranean was Egypt, where impressive monuments and artworks still offer a glimpse of the power and grandeur of one of the greatest empires of the ancient world. However, Egypt remained isolated and uninterested in extending itself much beyond the lands that border the Nile River. It was another group, the Persians, who inhabited the region now occupied by Iran, who first burst into prominence in the region. The Persians ultimately conquered Mesopotamia and extended Persia into Asia Minor (present-day Turkey).

The Persians were accomplished conquerors, and their continuing expansion brought them into conflict with the Greeks, inhabitants of the mountainous Balkan Peninsula. The Greeks traded with all the civilizations of the Mediterranean. They took the best ideas of these cultures and incorporated them into their own culture, improving them as they did so. Two invasions by the Persians ended in Greek victories and ushered in a great period of expansion and learning. Greek colonies spread throughout the Mediterranean. Greek philosophy and learning exploded; this was the time of Plato and Aristotle.

This map shows the Fertile Crescent, the area between the Tigris and Euphrates Rivers, in ancient Mesopotamia. The region is now the countries of Iraq, Syria, and Kuwait. Mesopotamia is regarded as a cradle of western civilization.

ALEXANDER THE GREAT'S MACEDONIAN EMPIRE

Eventually, the division between the various Greek city-states would be their downfall, even as the extraordinary ideas of Greek culture, known as Hellenism, continued to expand to the rest of the world. North of Greece, in a region called Macedonia, a warrior king named Phillip created a new army based around an improvement on traditional Greek fighting methods. He then used these methods to conquer all of Greece. But rather than destroy Greek culture, Phillip wanted to absorb it; he hired the philosopher Aristotle to be the tutor for his young son Alexander.

After Phillip's death by assassination in 336 BCE, Alexander took an army of Macedonians and Greeks on the most impressive invasion in history. With his fierce army, Alexander struck into Asia Minor, defeated and crushed the Persians, swept through Egypt and then Mesopotamia, and reached the outskirts of India before his weary soldiers forced him to turn back. These invasions forged an enormous empire.

Alexander, who is commonly known as Alexander the Great, did not live long enough to secure his Macedonian Empire, which collapsed almost

Alexander the Great was king of Macedon. Through his impressive and extended military campaigns, Alexander created one of the ancient world's largest and most influential empires.

At its height, the great Roman Empire extended 1,930 square miles (5 million square km), from parts of Europe to North Africa to the Middle East. The Roman Empire was so vast that it accounted for one fourth of the entire world's population.

immediately after his death from disease in 323 BCE. The greatest impact of Macedonia, however, was the spread of Greek culture, language, and learning throughout the Persian and Egyptian Empires that Alexander had conquered. Egypt would be ruled by Greeks until the time of the Roman Empire, as would large portions of the Persian Empire. Greek became the standard language of the eastern Mediterranean, a fact that not even the later Roman conquests could change.

THE RISE AND FALL OF THE ROMAN EMPIRE

It was the Romans who next strode onto the stage of the Mediterranean world. Like the Greeks, the Romans were geniuses at incorporating the best of the cultures they met into their own society; but unlike the Greeks, they had an excellence for organization and governing. From a single insignificant village in the middle of Italy (founded, according to legend, in 753 BCE), by about 150 BCE they had defeated all rivals for dominance in the Mediterranean and had conquered Greece itself.

If Alexander and the Macedonians spread Greek culture to the east, then it was the Romans who spread it to the west. Greek philosophy, poetry, and literature forged the foundation of Roman thought, profoundly influencing all aspects of their society.

However, even with their genius for government, the Romans could not solve the problems that were splitting their empire apart. After two centuries of peace, civil war and invasions by German barbarians from beyond the Rhine ultimately caused the collapse of the empire, and the last Roman emperor was killed in battle in 476 CE.

THE BYZANTINE EMPIRE AND THE BEDOUINS

The eastern half of the Roman Empire, however, survived, although it is usually referred to as the Byzantine

Empire after the fall of Rome, because the original name of its capital, Constantinople, was known as Byzantium.

The Byzantine Empire was largely Roman in name only since it remained isolated from western Europe and its language was Greek, not Latin. For centuries, however, the Byzantine Empire preserved the glory of the Greco-Roman civilization, although it was ultimately unable to revive it. Much of its history would instead be spent in defending itself against invasions from the east, especially from the Persians.

In the midst of this clash of empires, nomadic Arabs, or Bedouins, lived a traditional existence on the Arabian Peninsula. Well situated to conduct trade between Europe and Asia, Bedouins controlled the caravan routes from Syria to India and China and sailed ships up and down the Red Sea and the Persian Gulf.

At various times they had been under the leadership of the Persian, Roman, and Byzantine Empires, but at the end of the sixth century, war between Persia and Byzantium left them as they normally were—under no dominion, free to roam the inhospitable desert interior of Arabia. It would take the creation of a new religion, Islam, to unite this nomadic culture.

THE PROPHET MUHAMMAD AND THE REVELATION OF ISLAM

The prophet Muhammad was born in 571 CE in the city of Mecca, an important trading center in Arabia. As a young man he traveled widely into Syria on trading missions and became an accomplished merchant. He married Khadijah, a wealthy widow in 596. She bore him five children: four daughters and a son who died in infancy.

Muhammad was an intelligent man who liked to meditate and pray alone in a cave near Mecca. In 610, while meditating, he had a vision of the angel Gabriel, who spoke to him; this was the first of several revelations

Nomadic Arab tribes called Bedouin engaged in trade with a variety of cultures, from Europe to Asia, and had been subject to the rule of the changing empires. Finally, with the introduction of Islam, they were united under one culture.

ISLAM'S FIVE PILLARS

At the heart of Islam are the Five Pillars, the most fundamental beliefs that every Muslim shares. They are:

1. Belief in one God (*Shahadah*): Each Muslim is expected to profess his faith daily in a simple prayer: "there is no God but God (Allah) and Muhammad is his prophet."

2. Prayer (*Salah*): Five times a day (at sunrise, midday, mid-afternoon, sunset, and an hour after sunset) each Muslim is expected to recite prayers in Arabic. While it is best to do so in a mosque, it is not necessary; likewise, the worshipper should point himself toward Mecca if possible.

3. Charity (*Zakah*): Every Muslim is expected to give to charity with what he has after his basic needs have been met.

4. Fasting (*Sawm*): During the month of Ramadan, Muslims must not eat, drink, smoke, or have sexual relations between sunrise and sunset; in addition, they are told to avoid anger, greed, lust, and other vices. Muslims believe that they make these sacrifices to learn self-control and to remember the less fortunate; sharing in the fast also strengthens the bonds of community between Muslims around the world.

5. Pilgrimage (*Hajj*): At least once in their lifetime, Muslims are expected to make a pilgrimage to the holy city of Mecca in Saudi Arabia. Many traditions are involved in the Hajj, including the wearing of special garments that are the same for all worshippers, reminding them that everyone is the same in the eyes of God.

These Five Pillars are central to the belief of Sunni Muslims, the largest sect of Islam. Shia Muslims place less emphasis on them, although they practice all of the same fundamental beliefs.

that would form the basis of the Quran, the sacred holy book of the Muslims.

Over time, the revelations Muhammad received led him to form Islam, a new religion that was different from the idol worship then practiced by the Arabs of Mecca. Like Judaism and Christianity, Islam was and is a monotheistic religion, meaning that its followers believed in only one god instead of the many idols worshipped at the Kaaba, the black, cube-shaped temple in Mecca believed to have been created by Abraham. Muhammad also incorporated many of the traditions of Judaism and Christianity, proclaiming that he had received the final revelation of God that completed the prior revelations to Jews and Christians.

At first, Muhammad had only one follower, his wife Khadijah. Soon he converted his cousin to Islam and then his close friend Abu Bakr. Muhammad managed to convert a few others in secret and later began to preach publicly in 613. As can be expected, most people did not heed Muhammad's message, though he managed to gain enough followers and soon came into conflict with the rulers of Mecca. Much of the wealth of these leaders was based not only on their central location at the crossroads of many of Arabia's trade routes but on the fees paid by pilgrims to the

Kaaba. Muhammad's message that the gods whose idols were housed at the Kaaba were false threatened the rulers' profits and their control of Mecca. These rulers began a long period of persecuting the new converts of Islam, a term meaning "submission," to the will of Allah or God, who are called Muslims. Some Muslims immediately fled Mecca to Abyssinia (present-day Ethiopia), although many remained in Arabia with Muhammad.

In 622, with his own clan no longer protecting him, Muhammad and his followers left Mecca and traveled to Medina. Welcomed into the city, Muhammad helped end the strife between its rival clans, and many converted to Islam. This journey, called the *hjira*, marks the beginning of the Islamic calendar.

War soon began between the cities; Muhammad took advantage of a temporary truce in 628 to make a pilgrimage to Mecca, but hostilities soon broke out again. In 630 Muhammad returned at the head of a large army and the people of Mecca surrendered without a fight. Muhammad destroyed the idols in the Kaaba and made Mecca the center of the Muslim world. (Even today, devout Muslims continue the tradition of praying in the direction of Mecca five times a day no matter where they are on the globe.)

Two years later, in 632, Muhammad died, having begun a new faith that would soon spread throughout the Mediterranean world.

After the conquest of Mecca, Muslims were the dominant force in Arabia. In the remaining two years of Muhammad's life, the followers of Islam unified the region for the first time since the Romans had ruled it. Soon, Muslims began to spread Islam beyond its boundaries, sweeping into Syria and Mesopotamia. Inspired by Islam's message, exceptionally skilled in desert fighting, and mounted on the finest horses in the world, Muslim armies proved unstoppable. The exhaustion of the Byzantine and Persian Empires after their long wars created a void that Islam rushed to fill.

By 660 CE, thirty years after the death of Muhammad, Muslim armies had conquered Egypt and Persia and converted many of the people living

After conquering Mecca, Muhammad and his followers, said to be a force of ten thousand men, destroyed the idols he deemed false in the Kaaba. Muhammad then declared Mecca the center of the Muslim world.

there to Islam. The two most ancient empires in the Mediterranean had fallen almost without a fight to the Muslim warriors, leaving them in control of the ancient Mesopotamian region. Within one hundred years of Muhammad's death, Muslims had conquered all of North Africa. In the east they stood at the frontiers of India, and in the west, they prepared to invade Europe.

CHAPTER TWO

THE ARAB CAPITAL OF CÓRDOBA

The greatest city in western Europe in the tenth century was Córdoba, located in present-day Spain. In this capital city, Arab leaders called caliphs presided over courts of scholars whose names would later become famous not only in the Islamic world but all across Christian Europe. These brilliant minds studied ancient Greek scientists and philosophers and built on their knowledge to form their own scholarship.

But how did Córdoba become an Arab capital to rival the city that had once ruled the world? And how was it that Arabic, not Latin, was the language of its scholars? How had a sleepy Spanish town come to rival Baghdad, where the successors to the Prophet ruled over an empire that nearly equaled the expansive Roman world at its height? To understand the rise of Córdoba, one needs to first examine the history of Spain and its place in the Mediterranean world.

The great Carthaginian military commander Hannibal is best known for heroically crossing the Pyrenees and Alps with an army that included several elephants during the Second Punic War.

SPAIN'S EARLY HISTORY

Prior to the emergence of Islam in Arabia, various groups had moved into the Iberian Peninsula, the large boxy region of Europe that today includes Portugal and Spain, including the Celts, who dominated northern Europe until the rise of the Romans. By the ninth century BCE, three major groups dominated the Iberian region: the Celtic tribesmen in the interior, Greek colonies on the eastern Mediterranean coast, and Phoenician (a people originally from the region of present-day Lebanon who had created a large trading empire centered on the North African city Carthage) colonies on the southern coast.

Carthage's domination of the Mediterranean brought it into conflict with the Roman Empire, which fought a series of conflicts known as the Punic Wars (from the Latin word for Phoenician) from 264 BCE to 146 BCE. Spain played a key role in the second Punic War; the great Carthaginian general Hannibal led an army of forty thousand men and several elephants over the Pyrenees and the Alps and into Italy itself, where he defeated several Roman armies before eventually retreating to Carthage to defend it from a Roman invasion. Despite Hannibal's efforts, Carthage lost the second war and with it her Spanish colonies;

Rome would triumph in the third war, destroying the city of Carthage and assuming full mastery of the Mediterranean world.

For another two centuries the Romans struggled to complete their conquest of the Iberian Peninsula, battling the Celts, Greeks, and remaining Phoenicians until it was finally unified under their control during the reign of Augustus, the first Roman emperor. Spain quickly became one of empire's most important provinces. Its olive trees, first brought by the Greeks, were an important export then, as they are now. Eventually, the people of Spain were granted full Roman citizenship, an indication of how important the province was to the empire. The Roman emperor Trajan (whose magnificent column commemorating his victory over the Dacians still stands in Rome) was also born in Spain.

The Romans contributed greatly to Spain and Spanish culture. They built roads and aqueducts that still stand today. They offered the Latin language, the ancestor of modern Spanish. But perhaps the most important thing they brought to Spain, which would have a tremendous impact on its future history, was Christianity. First appearing in Spain in the second century CE, by the end of the Roman period Christianity was firmly established as the leading religion of Spain. In fact, in many regions of Spain it was the bishops of the early Christian church who preserved order when the Romans could no longer do so.

As the empire collapsed, the barbarians who had attacked it moved deeper into Roman territory and began to rule the former provinces as independent kingdoms. In many cases, the word *barbarian* is not entirely accurate. Many of the peoples from outside the borders of the empire had tried to acquire Roman culture and ways; they spoke Latin (or at least the educated among them did) and tried to emulate the grandeur of the Roman rulers. But in many ways they were very different. Instead of the regimented hierarchies of the Roman army and government, strong military leaders governed German tribes. Tribal and family loyalty was more important than an abstract concept of national unity. The Europe the barbarians ruled was very different from the stable ideal of *Pax Romana*, a Latin term meaning "the Roman peace" that the earlier Roman government had brought to the regions its leaders had conquered.

THE VISIGOTHS

The fifth century was a chaotic, unstable time for western Europe. The old Roman Imperial system was swept away by the barbarian invasions, but the

The Visigoths invaded Gaul and other cities of present-day France before moving on to Spain. Branches of the Goths had begun spreading during the late Roman Empire, and they ruled parts of Europe until the eighth century.

barbarians fought each other as well as with the Romans; warfare was nearly constant in some regions. Without the Roman army, banditry reappeared, and whole regions of Italy were devastated. Desperate for protection, the people of villages and towns turned to warlords and their armed bands to protect them. In many cases, barbarians provided this protection in exchange for support of the leader and his men. Before long, the system of feudalism arose from these basic relationships and bargains that dominated European government for the next one thousand years.

Around the 460s, Spain was fully conquered by a Germanic people known as the Visigoths, a name meaning "West Goths." Capturing the region more or less intact (with only a small part of the peninsula held by the Byzantine Empire), they at first ruled Spain from the city of Toulouse (in present-day France) until they were driven out of the region by another Germanic tribe, the Franks. Establishing a new capital at the city of Toledo, the Visigoths consolidated their power until they ruled the largest unified kingdom in western Europe.

The Visigoths ruled Spain, but, as outsiders, they were forced to rely upon their military strength in order to maintain order. Two factors kept their leadership relatively weak, however. First, the Visigoths elected their king from the highest-ranking nobles, which led to frequent struggles for the crown. Second, their lack of a governing system left controlling such a large kingdom extremely difficult. (Because of this lack of government, the Visigoths frequently relied upon the church to help them run the country. This reliance upon the church for control is among the reasons why religion became so crucial to Spain.)

However, the Visigoths were also responsible for many achievements. As noted earlier, Spain was the largest Christian kingdom in Europe at the time. In the seventh century, a single legal code, which combined elements of Roman law and German traditions, was put into place throughout the kingdom. This was a major advance that was centuries ahead of how the rest of Europe was governed. And Spain remained a rich region, vital to Mediterranean commerce, a fact that later attributed to its downfall.

THE ROCK OF GIBRALTAR

Across the Straits of Gibraltar, in the regions of Africa we today call Morocco, Algeria, and Libya, there lived a nomadic people called the Berbers who inhabited a harsh desert region known as the Mahgreb. They are and were a tough people, well adapted to living in the desert and preserving their nomadic heritage. They had fought against the Romans, who had called the region Mauritania or "the Land of the Moors," which is what the Spanish called them.

As Islam spread into North Africa, it came in contact with these peoples and converted many of them, extending the rule of the caliphs, as the successors of Muhammad were called, farther west along the Mediterranean. Soon bands of Arabs and Moors were raiding the southern coast of Spain, forming an intimate connection that the two regions would continue to share for the next seven hundred years.

In 710 CE, a dispute broke out between the family of the previous king and Rodrigo, a powerful duke who had seized the throne for himself. Rodrigo's opponents appealed to Musa ibn-Nusair, the ruler of the Moors. He sent his best general, Tariq Ibn Zayid, with a small army, across the Straits of Gibraltar and into southern Spain. They landed near an enormous mountain of

rock that Tariq named after himself: Jeebal Tariq—Tariq's Rock, or as we know it, the Rock of Gibraltar.

If Rodrigo's opponents had hoped that the Moors were simply on another raid and would leave as soon as they had defeated the king, they were mistaken. In 711, at the battle of Guadalete, Tariq's army decisively beat the Spaniards and killed Rodrigo; the entire Visigoth kingdom of Spain was left defenseless. The Moors had not come to share the region; they had come to conquer it.

THE UMAYYAD

The conquest of Spain proceeded with the same incredible speed that had characterized the earlier Muslim conquests of Arabia, Persia, and North Africa. By 719, almost the entire Iberian Peninsula was under the control of the Moors.

Rodrigo, the last Visigoth king, was defeated by the Moors in 711 at the Battle of Guadalete. In just a few years, most of the Iberian Peninsula was controlled by Moors, who continued to try to conquer even more land.

RODRIGO'S LEGEND

Many legends exist about the fall of Spain to the Moors. One of the best known concerns the last Visigoth king of Spain, Rodrigo. According to the legend, two old men came to visit the king in Toledo, his capital city, one day. They told him that there was an enchanted tower nearby the city, with a heavy iron gate; and on that gate were many locks. For the tower contained a terrible secret that would bring destruction on anyone who knew it; because of this, each king had added his own lock to the tower, twenty-seven in all, and no one had ever tried to pass the gate.

Rodrigo, being brash and arrogant, immediately left with his entire court and went to the tower. He made the two old men open all the locks, and then he stepped inside. Beyond the entrance he found a giant statue made of metal that swung a heavy mace all around, striking the ground with all its might. But Rodrigo saw the words "I only do my duty" stamped on its chest, and when he told it that he merely wanted to learn the secret of the tower, it stopped and allowed him to pass. He went up long flights of stairs until he came to a room at the top of the tower.

In this room was a casket studded with gems. Rodrigo opened it and found a single piece of parchment. On it was painted a picture of two Moors on horseback, with scimitars (curved Arabian swords) and bows, and above them was written "Behold, rash man, those who shall hurl thee from thy throne and subdue thy kingdom."

There was only one small section of the far north, along the Atlantic coast, where a Christian state survived. This was the tiny kingdom of Asturias, founded by a survivor of the battle of Guadalete. The modern Spanish state would one day emerge from this small Christian outpost, but that day was more than eight hundred years away. The Moors continued to press on into Europe, storming over the Pyrenees to invade France, where they actually conquered some of the region around Toulouse; but in 732, the Franks, under the leadership of Charles Martel (the grandfather of Charlemagne) defeated them soundly at Poitiers; after that, the Moors were content to rule the Iberian Peninsula and did not attempt further invasions of France.

At the time of the Moorish conquest, the Islamic world was ruled from Damascus, the ancient city in Syria. During that period, Damascus was home to the Umayyad family, who had assumed the leadership of the Islamic world after a struggle with the followers of Muhammad's nephew Ali in the 650s. (This conflict ultimately led to the split between Sunni Muslims and Shia Muslims, who followed Ali and believed that the Prophet had intended him to be his successor.) The Umayyad caliphs appointed governors, or emirs, to

Though much of the Umayyad dynasty was extinguished when it was overthrown by the Abbasids, the Umayyad prince Abd-ar-Rahman went on to rule al-Andalus. His descendants continued to rule the region for centuries.

rule over Spain (which was considered part of the province of North Africa, including Morocco), but their actual power was weak.

In 750, however, the Umayyads themselves were overthrown by another family, the Abbasids, who moved the capital from Damascus to Baghdad, a city in Persia (present-day Iraq). Although most of the Umayyad family was killed by the Abbasids, one Umayyad prince, Abd-ar-Rahman, survived. He made his way to Spain, arriving in 756, and quickly established himself as the sole ruler of the region. For the next 300 years descendents of Abd-ar-Rahman would rule Spain, or al-Andalus as they called it. In 929, Abd-ar-Rahman III would take the title of caliph for himself, challenging the Abbasids for dominance in the Western Mediterranean—for he was ruler not just of al-Andalus, the Muslim region of Spain, but the North African territories from which the Moors had invaded. As a symbol of the splendor of the caliphate, Abd-ar-Rahman constructed a new city, Medinat al-Zahra, on a mountain near Córdoba to serve as the administrative center of his government, and it was here that Albucasis was born in 936.

ALBUCASIS'S CÓRDOBA

The caliphate of Córdoba would become one of the most advanced states in either Europe or the Islamic world. Scientists and philosophers to rival any of those in Baghdad lived and worked in al-Andalus. While the great works of antiquity were quietly forgotten in a Europe riddled with plague and often more concerned with day-to-day survival, in al-Andalus they survived and were kept and copied in Arabic with great reverence. Every educated man in al-Andalus possessed a library that would have shamed even the rulers of France and Germany.

The Great Mosque of Córdoba is a visual reminder of the history of the region. Originally constructed on the site of the Visgoths' demolished Catholic basilica, the mosque was converted to a Catholic church when Córdoba returned to Christian rule.

The caliphate was advanced in other ways as well, especially when it came to the tolerance of religions other than Islam. While in Europe heretics were burned, Jews discriminated against and forced to live apart from Christians, and Muslims the target of attacks and reprisals, in al-Andalus there was truce between these religious groups. Jews held high positions in the government of the caliphate, while Christians were allowed to practice their religion more or less unmolested; indeed, Toledo had a bishop, who served as an important go-between in the caliphate and the Holy Roman Empire.

The greatest symbol of the power of the caliphate was its capital city, Córdoba, and the greatest monument in Córdoba was its mosque, known as the Mezquita. This enormous structure, the largest mosque in Spain, took more than two hundred years to construct. After the fall of Córdoba in 1236, the Spanish, whose numerous changes marred tragically the mosque's once beautiful architecture, turned it into a Christian church.

Only in a place of such fabulous learning and achievement, where gold flowed like rivers, could a climate rich enough for true advancement of science arise. Albucasis's skill was so great that at about twenty-five years of age he became the court physician for al-Hakim II, the ruler of al-Andalus from 961–976. Albucasis was soon the greatest physician of the Middle Ages, with a fame destined to eclipse that of even the great doctors of the ancient world.

But to understand why Albucasis was so important and revolutionary, we must first examine the body of knowledge that he inherited from the ancient Greeks and Romans. Albucasis himself expressed his admiration and respect of the ancient Greek and Roman physicians when he wrote, "What ever I know, I owe solely to my assiduous reading of books of the ancients, to my desire to understand them and to appropriate this science; then I have added the observation and experience of my whole life."

CHAPTER THREE

PHYSICIANS OF THE ANCIENT WORLD

Medicine in the ancient world was quite different from what it is today. The Egyptians were some of the first physicians, but they were also immersed in superstition. Although they were able to treat many diseases that affected the outside of the body, such as the skin and the eyes, they could do little or nothing for internal ailments except resort to magic spells. Although physicians in ancient Egypt were not priests, they were trained at temples where they learned about the use of many drugs, including some still in use today.

The greatest early Egyptian physician was Imhotep (about 2650–2600 BCE), the architect and mathematician who designed the first pyramid. Oddly enough, although embalming was an advanced art in Egypt (as shown by the many mummies that survive today), the Egyptians were not well versed in anatomy. It is for this reason that they attempted only the most basic of surgical procedures.

Imhotep was an Egyptian physician, as well as an architect and engineer. He is often shown in this pose with a shaven head and a piece of papyrus on his knees.

The Mesopotamians also believed in magic, but they showed a surprisingly advanced interest in studying the course and symptoms of diseases. They used a wide variety of drugs and other remedies and emphasized the role of rest and diet in restoring health. They had a more advanced knowledge of anatomy than the Egyptians had. Physicians in Mesopotamia were still considered a kind of magician, however, as the study of dreams was an important part in their diagnosis.

MEDICAL SCIENCE IN ANCIENT GREECE

Greek medicine too arose out of superstition. Healing was associated with temples, especially of the gods Apollo and Aesculapius (the god of medicine). Pilgrims would journey to these temples to receive cures, at first from priests, then later from physicians associated with the temple and called the Sons of Aesculapius or Asclepiadae. These temple physicians, who were not themselves priests, were the origin of the world's first true physicians.

The unique Greek capacity for synthesizing ideas from other cultures can be seen in the emergence of their medical science. Many of the drugs and treatments that the early Greek physicians utilized had originated in Egypt, whose culture had a distinct influence on the Greeks as demonstrated in their art. However, other ideas were purely Greek in origin and show profound capacity for logical thought that is the hallmark of this important and influential people.

From the start, we can observe the use of reason to analyze and diagnose illnesses. Pilgrims who traveled to the Greek healing centers had to prepare by fasting, cleaning themselves, and praying; their dreams were interpreted by the priests—but the prescription was usually to change the patient's diet. This emphasis on diet would remain one of the most important characteristics of Greek medicine. What is important about this process is that each patient's symptoms were studied and compared to other sufferers. In this way, specific diseases began to be identified and treatments for them discovered. This process was aided by the early philosophers, such as Pythagoras, who took a great interest in the study of medicine.

Eventually the first medical schools evolved out of the temple schools that instructed the Asclepiadae. The most famous of these was at Cos, an island in the Aegean Sea near the coast of Turkey. This place was famous not only for its shrine to Aesculapius but because it was home to Hippocrates (460–377 BCE), the most influential physician in the history of Europe.

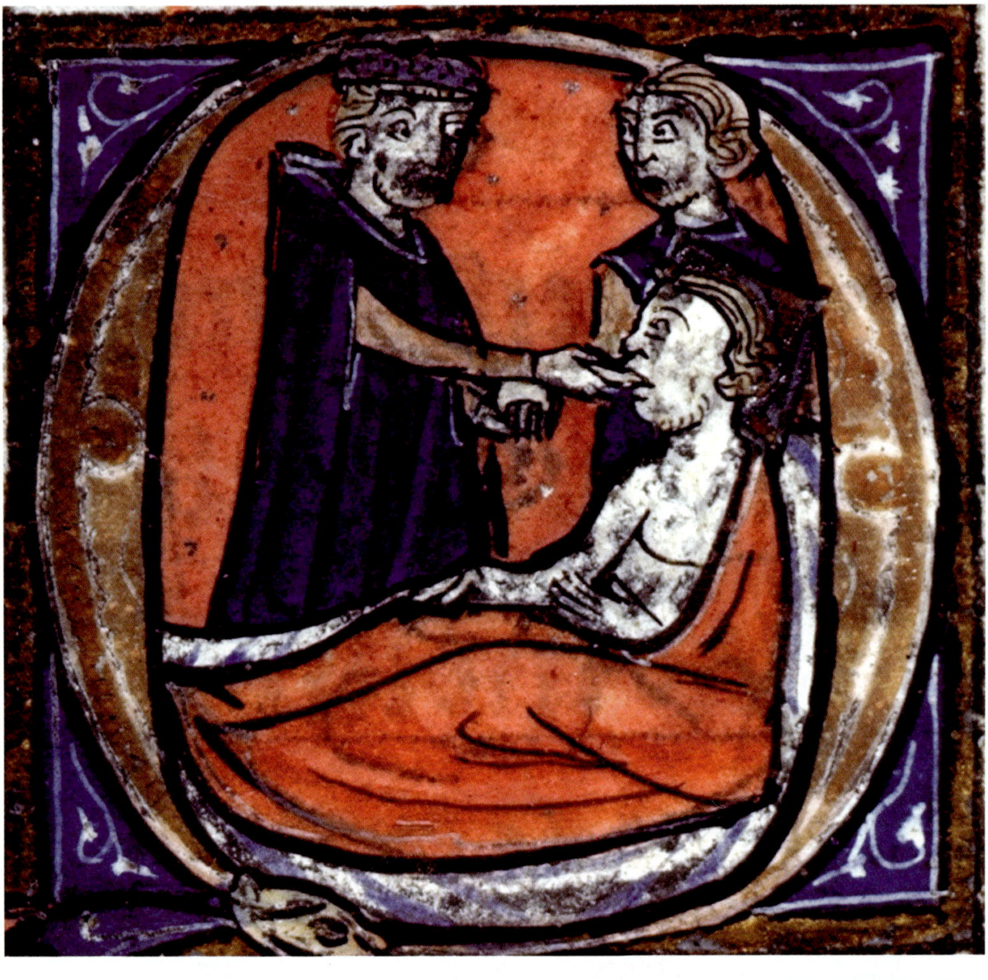

Considered to be the "Father of Western Medicine," Hippocrates was the first physician to place an emphasis on observing a patient's symptoms before diagnosis. The Hippocratic Oath that physicians take today was written by Hippocrates or one of his students.

Hippocrates was born on Cos, and it was he who first broke the chains of superstition that bound medical study. His basic principles form the basis of all medical research to the present day.

Hippocrates was the first physician to stress the overwhelming importance of observing a patient's symptoms first before deciding what caused them. By diagnosing diseases in this way, they could be described by their symptoms and not their causes (which would have been inaccurate in any case, as the germ theory of disease was 1,500 years in the future). Before Hippocrates, physicians came up with a cause—anything from divine wrath to ingesting the wrong kind of food—and then tried to fit a patient's symptoms into this pattern. Hippocrates reversed this process instead of diagnosing a patient's illness by seeing how his or her symptoms fit in with the symptoms of other patients and identifying the disease in that fashion.

Hippocrates also introduced the idea that whatever a patient revealed to a physician should not be revealed to anyone else—a practice enshrined in the famous oath attributed to him. He stressed cleanliness in a physician and insisted that he should always wash his hands before treating anyone. He identified many diseases that still plague the world, such as pneumonia, typhus, tuberculosis, and arthritis.

THE HIPPOCRATIC OATH

The Hippocratic oath is attributed to the brilliant Greek physician Hippocrates, known as the "Father of Medicine." Traditionally, his students swore it when they completed their training. Today, doctors continue to take this oath when they graduate medical school.

OATH OF HIPPOCRATES:

"Above All, Do No Harm"

I swear by Apollo the physician, and Aesculapius, and Hygeia, and Panacea and all the gods and goddesses, making them my witnesses, that I will fulfill, according to my ability and judgment, this Oath and covenant:

To hold him, who has taught me this art, as equal to my parents, and to live my life in partnership with him, and if he is in need of money to give him a share of mine, and to regard his offspring as equal to my brothers in male lineage, and to teach them this art—if they desire to learn it—without fee and covenant; to give a share of precepts and oral instruction and all the other learning to my sons and to the sons of him who has instructed me, and to pupils who have signed the covenant and who have taken an oath according to the medical law, but to no one else.

I will apply dietetic measures for the benefit of the sick according to my ability and judgment; I will keep them from harm and injustice.

I will neither give a deadly drug to anybody if asked for it, nor will I make a suggestion to this effect. Similarly I will not give to a woman an abortive remedy. In purity and holiness, I will guard my life and my art.

I will not use the knife, not even on sufferers from stone, but will withdraw in favor of such men as are [skilled] in this work.

Whatever houses I may visit, I will come for the benefit of the sick, remaining free of all intentional injustice, of all mischief, and in particular of sexual relations with both male and female persons, be they free or slaves.

What I may see or hear in the course of treatment or even outside of the treatment in regard to the life of men, which on no account [ought to be] spread abroad, I will keep to myself, holding such things shameful to be spoken about.

If I fulfill this Oath and do not violate it, may it be granted to me to enjoy life and art, being honored with fame among all men for all time to come; if I transgress it and swear falsely, may the opposite of all this be my lot.

Hippocrates strongly believed in the human body's ability to heal itself. He stressed moderation in all things—in eating, drinking, and exercising. Most of his treatments involved treating the symptoms and relieving the suffering of the patient while the disease ran its course—a surprisingly advanced and practical outlook, given that antibiotics lay far in the future.

Hippocrates's real contribution to the art of medicine was that he brought a systematic, logical approach to the study of disease. His followers spread his ideas all through the Greek world, and they followed Alexander into the Middle East. The Romans took up the practice of Hippocratic medicine as well, until it was established throughout the Mediterranean. A large body of writing, *The Corpus Hippocraticum*, attributed to Hippocrates but probably written by his followers, remained part of the medical curriculum well into the nineteenth century.

Other Greeks were also interested in the study of medicine. Many philosophers studied it as part of their attempt to understand the whole of human experience; the greatest of these, Aristotle (384–322 BCE), although not a physician himself, made important medical contributions through his dissections of animals. He is considered the "Father of Comparative Anatomy," since his studies of the anatomy of animals helped the Greeks gain insight into how the human body functions. (His animal anatomy study was specifically useful in the early field of embryology, since he made many observations about the stages of developments of chick embryos.)

CLAUDIUS GALEN BUILDS ON HIPPOCRATES

The next great contributor to Greek medicine was Claudius Galen of Pergamum (131–201 CE). Pergamum, in present-day Bergama, Greece, was a city that had been founded centuries before by Greek immigrants to Asia Minor. Although he preferred to speak Greek for most of his life (perhaps for effect, as Greek was considered a more "learned" language than Latin at the time), Galen was a Roman citizen and eventually was a physician to four emperors.

As a young man, Galen studied several subjects until settling on medicine, which would turn out to be his true calling. He spent several years traveling to many cities throughout the Greek world to study including Smyrna, Corinth, and Alexandria, the city in Egypt that had been founded by Alexander the Great and was home to the greatest collection of scholars and manuscripts in the ancient world. By

157 he returned to Pergamum, working as a physician for a gladiatorial school. And it was here that Galen acquired valuable knowledge about the nature and treatment of wounds.

Galen's work in Pergamum eventually led him to Rome, where his fame as a physician and writer eventually got him appointed as the court doctor to the emperor Marcus Aurelius. But it was his work as a writer and experimenter that caused Galen to be the dominant voice in medicine for some 1,200 years.

Galen voraciously devoured the works of Hippocrates and published them with his own annotations. He eventually wrote twenty-two volumes on medical literature, which codified

This artwork depicts Galen assisting a wounded gladiator. The ancient Greek physician learned much about wounds and injuries in this capacity. His medical research and writing were later studied by many scientists of the Islamic world.

and preserved Hippocratic thinking for centuries. He seized upon the concept of the body's four humors, or fluids, (blood, black bile, yellow bile, and phlegm) that at the time were believed to control the body's functioning. Although he used this theory to explain the causes of many diseases, it has since been disproved. Because he believed in the concept of the four humors and that a disproportionate ratio of humors in the human body often resulted in disease, Galen especially advocated the use of bloodletting, draining blood from patients, and purging, inducing vomiting, as treatments.

However, Galen made many positive contributions to medical science. He dissected both living and dead animals, studying their internal structures in order to learn how similar structures worked in human beings. He was the first physician to prove that the arteries and veins carried blood, not air as had been previously thought. He believed that the source of thought was the brain, not the heart as Aristotle and others had believed. He identified the major nerves of the body and performed some of the earliest tests on them.

Although he was not a Christian, Galen followed the belief of some Greek philosophers that there was a single creator of the world. Because of this, he was acceptable to later Christian and Muslim thinkers who might otherwise have dismissed him as a pagan and not worthy of reading. This fact preserved much of his work to the present day.

Although Galen was in many ways a brilliant scientist who was far ahead of his time, in other ways he failed the spirit of his great master, Hippocrates. Although he made many strides in exploring human anatomy, he was also content to assert his ideas as facts without finding any evidence to support them. For example, Galen assumed that a structure called the *rete mirabile*, a complex jumble of blood vessels that exists in many hoofed animals, must exist in the neck of humans because he had observed it in sheep; however, humans do not in fact have this structure. This was bad enough, but he assigned many important functions to this nonexistent organ.

Although Galen thought that blood was vital to human life—he associated it with the pneuma, or life force—he made several errors in describing how it flowed through the human body. Galen believed that blood was not circulated but merely accumulated in the body (this was also why he endorsed bloodletting to remove the supposed excesses of blood that he felt caused diseases). He thought that the heart sucked blood into it from the veins and that the arteries were responsible for pumping blood through themselves.

He had only a rudimentary understanding of how the lungs passed air into the body, although he did understand that this was the reason that arterial blood was bright red and venous blood was bluish.

Galen's success and brilliance was as an organizer of the Hippocratic method into a system that was superior to any other system of medicine in the ancient world. His techniques lived on and were a profound influence on later Islamic physicians, especially Albucasis. Galen was willing to examine diseases and to try and find their causes. Unlike Hippocrates, Galen preferred to reason from a supposed cause to an effect. His system lasted for 1,000 years because of its effectiveness; but at the cost of stifling further research into the real causes of human illnesses.

Galen lived at the height of the Roman Empire. After his death in 201, the empire began its long decline toward its ultimate demise in the fifth century. The centuries that followed the fall of the Roman Empire were responsible for the complete stagnation (and in many cases, total loss) of medical and scientific knowledge in Europe. It would be left up to the rising new power of Islam to expand medical knowledge, and in the five centuries after the birth of Muhammad, several Muslims would be considered among the greatest physicians in history.

CHAPTER FOUR

MEDICINE IN THE ISLAMIC WORLD

In the first five hundred years after Muhammad, the Islamic world was in many ways forward looking, progressive, and scientifically advanced. Conversely, in the west, scientific advancement had slowed to a crawl. In the Islamic world, caliphs assembled courts of scholars who studied and built on ancient Greek philosophy. In the western world, European popes decided what their clergy would learn.

How was it that these Muslims had a closer relationship with the greatest works of antiquity than the successors to the Roman Empire had? Why did the Islamic world produce so many intellectuals and scientists during a period when knowledge was declining in Europe? To answer these questions, and to understand how it was that Spain produced the single greatest physician not only of the Middle Ages but since the days of antiquity, we must return to the early days of the Muslim conquests.

Conquering a region often meant destroying its culture that did not conform to the rules of the new rulers. Legend has it that Caliph Omar ordered the magnificent library of Alexandria to be destroyed. With that, many great works were lost.

THE ISLAMIC WORLD IN THE MIDDLE AGES

When the forces of the Prophet swept into Syria, they were entering a region of the world that had been thoroughly Hellenized since the time of Alexander the Great. Then a part of the Byzantine Empire, Syria remained a treasure trove of Greek knowledge and learning, although by this time some of it had been deliberately ignored by Christians, who considered some of the work of the Greeks to be contrary to Christian doctrine.

Muslims, too, would reject some Greek learning as unsuitable for the faithful. But in other areas, especially medicine (which had obvious importance to a nomadic people engaged in nearly perpetual warfare), they eagerly devoured the wisdom of the Greek world.

Further expansion into Mesopotamia merely increased Muslim access to Greek works, as these regions had also been part of both Alexander the Great's Macedonian Empire and the Roman and Byzantine Empires. Moreover, the Muslim conquests brought the Islamic world into contact with two other ancient civilizations: Persia and India.

Although Persia had never regained the preeminence it had enjoyed in the fifth century BCE, it remained a civilization of great sophistication and its power was still strong

When Muslim warriors entered India, little did they know the Islamic world would benefit from much of the culture and knowledge there. For instance, the Indian people were well versed in using plants and herbs as medicines.

in the region. Contact with Persia was a shock that permanently changed the Islamic world (and laid the groundwork for some lasting conflicts, as Persia would ultimately become a Shia region while Arabia and much of the rest of the Muslim regions would remain Sunni). Persian art, literature, and poetry permeated and influenced the Muslim world. Before long, the love of learning and knowledge that the Persian rulers had inspired at their court became the model that the caliphs used to rule their own empire. The ideal Muslim prince was no longer just a fierce mounted warrior; after contact with the Persians, he was also expected to be a poet and scholar.

On the frontiers of Persia the warriors of Islam entered India, eventually subduing most of the northwest region of the subcontinent and converting it to Islam—the area of present-day Pakistan. The people of India also made important contributions to Islamic science and medicine, especially in the study of various medicinal herbs and drugs. The medical tradition founded by the Arab conquerors of northern India is still practiced there to this day.

These changes to the Muslim world produced an age of great philosophers, men who advanced human knowledge not only about the treatment of diseases but also in mathematics, physics, and chemistry.

In medicine, this would culminate in the work of Albucasis, but he built upon a foundation of many other important thinkers.

THE GREATEST PHILOSOPHER OF AL-ANDALUS

The Persian philosopher and physician Abu Bakr Muhammad Ibn Zakariya al-Razi, known in the West by his Latin name, Rhazes (or Rasis), lived between 865 and 925. Like Galen, he had pursued many studies before becoming a physician, including being a jeweler, money-changer, lute-player, and alchemist. Problems with his vision led him to seek medical treatment and then apply his formidable mind to the practice of medicine.

Rhazes was widely read in the Greek philosophers and physicians, and he incorporated much of their thinking into his own; but more important, he followed their example of examining evidence empirically and using reason to understand the actual causes of events. Rhazes was a great experimenter and a careful observer of physical and biological phenomena. A prolific writer, he wrote more than one hundred books on alchemy, philosophy, and medicine; one of these is *Doubts About Galen*, where he finds fault with the great Greek physician in many areas, including the theory of

Among other disciplines, most notably medicine, a field to which he contributed greatly, Rhazes studied alchemy. This science was an early form of chemistry based on the idea that metals could be converted into gold to cure disease.

the humors. More important, he correctly realized that in many places Galen had presented theories as facts without any evidence to back them.

Rhazes also made several other important contributions to medical knowledge, including identifying measles and smallpox as separate diseases, the identification of asthma as a disease, and a study of seasonal allergies. He was the first to realize that fever was a defense mechanism of the body and a natural part of its fight against disease. He also was an accomplished chemist and pharmacist; not only did he gather together lists of known drugs and publish them together, he also introduced many treatments of his own, was the first to use opium as an anesthetic, discovered sulfuric acid, and perfected or created many of the tools of the pharmacists' trade, such as the mortar and pestle. In his injunction that a physician must also be a philosopher—today we would say "scientist"—we see a revival of the true spirit of Hippocratic inquiry that had been lost after Galen.

AVICENNA'S CONTRIBUTIONS TO MEDICINE

Another important Muslim physician and philosopher—and one who had a direct influence on Albucasis—was

UNDER THE INFLUENCE: AVERROES

The great Muslim physician and philosopher Abu al-Walid Muhammad ibn Ahmad ibn Rushd, known as Ibn Rushd to the Muslim world and Averroes to the West, was one of the greatest geniuses produced by al-Andalus. His works gained him great esteem in Europe, where he was considered one of the most important philosophers of the Middle Ages.

Born in 1126 near Córdoba, he was the son and grandson of important Islamic judges. As a young man he studied philosophy, medicine, and Islamic law. Eventually he would become both a judge and a physician.

In the West, Averroes is best known for his commentaries on Aristotle. Legend has it that one night he had a long conversation with Abu Ya'qub Yusuf, the ruler of Córdoba. Averroes so impressed the emir with his knowledge of Greek philosophy that he asked him to write about Aristotle. Averroes spent the rest of his life on this project, which preserved a treasure trove of ancient Greek writings that might otherwise have been lost forever.

Although he is chiefly remembered as a philosopher and judge, like so many of the great minds of the Muslim world Averroes also worked as a physician, having been appointed to be the personal physician to Abu Yaqub Yusuf. He wrote a major work on the subject, *al-Kulliyyat* (roughly, Generalities). He leaned heavily on the works of Galen but also added his own unique philosophical perspective.

Averroes is another outstanding example of the influence that the great minds of al-Andalus had on the development of medieval thought in Western Europe and also of how closely related the disciplines of philosophy and medicine were in the Islamic world.

Abu Ali al-Husain ibn Abdallah ibn Sina, known in the Arabic-speaking world as Ibn Sina and in the West by his Latin name, Avicenna. He was a child prodigy who had memorized the Quran by the age of ten and was a practicing physician by the age of eighteen. As a physician he made many important advances, developing his own treatments for illnesses. But his true interests lay in philosophy. He read the *Metaphysics of Aristotle* so many times that he memorized it. His works on logic and philosophy are almost unmatched by any other Muslim scholar.

In the West, however, Avicenna is best remembered for his work in medicine, which was comparable and in some ways surpassed the work of Rhazes. He recognized that tuberculosis was an infectious disease, a realization that Europe would not accept until the nineteenth century. His massive book, the fourteen-volume *Canons of Medicine*, was a standard reference text in Europe and the Middle East until well into the seventeenth century. His other writings also achieved some prominence in the West, especially his commentaries on Aristotle.

Persian scientist and philosopher Avicenna was one of the greatest minds of Islam's golden age. His masterwork, *Canons in Medicine*, was considered the gold standard of medical text for generations later throughout the medieval period.

CHAPTER FIVE

ALBUCASIS'S ACHIEVEMENTS

The man we know as Albucasis would have been influenced by all of the aforementioned works of medieval Arab scientists. Albucasis was from Medinat al-Zahra, the administrative city built by the first caliph of Córdoba, Abd-ar-Rahman. Because of the destruction of al-Zahra in 1010, we know relatively little about his life, though we know it was remarkable due to the many advances he made in surgical medicine.

Albucasis served as the royal physician to the court of one of the later caliphs, al-Hakim II, and had many students. He was probably of Spanish, not Arabian descent—one of the Spanish converts to Islam who was an important middle tier of Islamic society in al-Andalus.

ALBUCASIS'S METHOD OF MEDICINE

Albucasis practiced all kinds of medicine and developed many new techniques. His life's work was a comprehensive encyclopedia of medicine, perhaps the greatest work of its kind written during the Middle Ages, the *al-Tasrif liman 'Azija 'an al-Ta'lif* (usually called *The Method of Medicine*, although the literal translation is *An Aid to him that Lacks the Capacity to Read Big Books*, probably a reference to the lengthy writings of Avicenna). Although only the last volume, which was dedicated to surgery, became widely known in the West, the work as a whole is truly remarkable and details techniques that would be unknown or uncommon in the rest of Europe for centuries.

What all commentators agree on is that the variety of medical techniques and methods that Albucasis wrote about in the *al-Tasrif* is truly amazing. Indeed, had he been a Christian of the fifteenth century instead of a Muslim of the tenth, he would be remembered today as a true "Renaissance Man." The book seems to have been written as a practical guide to his students, whom he refers to as "my children," and expressed concern about their welfare.

Like Avicenna, Albucasis believed that a doctor had to closely observe his patient. Reviving the spirit of Hippocratic medicine, he urged that doctors behave ethically toward their patients, and he denounced quacks or physicians who offered treatments of doubtful use in return for money.

This illustration, from a fourteenth-century translation of *On Surgery* by Albucasis, shows sick men being observed by a doctor. *On Surgery* was the most read and most influential of the books of Albucasis's *al-Tasrif*.

Perhaps the most valuable thing about *al-Tasrif* is that it is a record of more than fifty years of the treatments provided by a gifted physician. The case histories, and the way that Albucasis interpreted these cases to make his diagnoses, show that the rational inquiry into the causes and treatment of diseases begun by Hippocrates still survived in the Islamic world.

Almost every possible medical condition is touched upon in the *al-Tasrif*. But Albucasis was not content to merely record the details he observed in humans. Like Aristotle and Galen, he also dissected animals to compare their internal structures with humans, but as an accomplished surgeon, his understanding of the human body far surpassed both Aristotle and Galen.

A VARIETY OF SPECIALTIES

Unlike today, when physicians specialize in a single branch of medicine, medieval physicians were well versed in most areas of practice. Albucasis made important contributions to nearly every field of medicine. He was very concerned about the successful delivery of babies, or what is now referred to as the field of obstetrics. He is the first person to describe Walcher's position, one in which the woman arches her back and has her knees on the edge of the table; this sometimes helps to make delivery easier. Albucasis was known for training midwives to ensure that they would deliver healthy babies.

Albucasis was very interested in the care of the joints and bones, or orthopedics. In addition to his writings on the surgery of these areas, he described what we know today as Kocher's technique. This method is used for repairing a dislocated shoulder by careful application of leverage to the dislocated arm while the patient is lying on his or her side. (The West would not rediscover this technique until the late nineteenth century.) He also described the technique of patellectomy, or the removal of the knee bone in cases when it has been smashed; this would not be reintroduced to the West until 1937. Albucasis also wrote about methods to set bones in simple and compound fractures.

Nearly alone among the physicians of the ancient and medieval world, Albucasis was very interested in dentistry. He described many different dental problems such as misaligned teeth and suggests ways to correct the flaws. He demonstrated techniques to reimplant teeth that had been knocked out of the mouth. He also described how to make artificial dentures out of the bones of animals.

Albucasis's interest in medicine was comprehensive and far reaching. He had a rare interest in dentistry. This illustration is taken from the Quran.

Albucasis was also among the first physicians in Europe to practice plastic surgery. The *al-Tasrif* describes several methods of plastic and reconstructive surgery that are still practiced today. He used ink to mark where to make incisions on the faces of his patients, for example; he also described methods of performing breast reduction surgery on women in procedures that greatly resemble the techniques that are still in use today.

SURGERY

Albucasis made his chief contributions to medicine in the field of surgery. The entire last volume of *al-Tasrif* is dedicated to the subject, and it is the most detailed work of its kind to have been written in the Middle Ages. In its meticulous description, accuracy, and inventiveness, *al-Tasrif* far outstrips any previous work and demonstrates a level of technique unknown prior to Albucasis, even among the Greek masters.

Albucasis was also a practical surgeon. As noted above, he was interested in repairing damaged joints. He also perfected techniques to remove arrows and heal other wounds.

The urinary system was often of particular interest to Islamic physicians, who would examine a patient's urine as a way to diagnose his or her illness. Albucasis carried this examination to a much higher level. He perfected surgical techniques to the bladder, kidney, and gallstones. Among the many surgical instruments he invented was a device to examine the urethra, the passage through which urine is expelled, a version of which is still in use today.

Albucasis was the first surgeon to successfully operate on the bowels. He also developed the innovative use of silk and catgut (tough thread made from the intestines of sheep) to stitch wounds shut.

The nervous system was also a curious part of the body to Albucasis, who described many different conditions caused by head and spinal injuries. He developed special tools for drilling into the skull without damaging the brain. He instructed other surgeons to pay particular attention to the anatomy of the skull in order to understand the proper surgical technique to avoid nerve damage. He demonstrated techniques to heal spinal fractures.

Albucasis was also interested in what today we call otorhinolaryngology, or treatment of the ears, nose, eyes, and throat. He knew how to set and heal fractures of the nasal bones. He also performed delicate surgeries on the ear and developed tools to examine and operate on the ear. He detailed how to do tracheotomies and extracted cataracts.

Albucasis showed an unusual concern for illnesses of women. He was the first physician to describe surgery to treat breast cancer. As noted before, he was able to do surgery to treat gallstones, but he made special note in *al-Tasrif* on how to respect the modesty of women when treating them for this condition. As mentioned before, Albucasis was an accomplished obstetrician, but he also practiced gynecology. One of his most important contributions to the art of medicine was the first use of a mirror to reflect light on a patient during an operation. He developed this technique to examine the cervixes of his female patients.

In addition to his many surgical techniques, Albucasis developed various surgical instruments, some of which are in use today. He may have even invented the humble tongue depressor. He is also credited with the creation of tooth extractors, obstetric devices (including forceps), a hook to remove nasal polyps, syringes to perform enemas, and various surgical knives and saws.

Albucasis identified hemophilia as a hereditary disease; he also perfected the use of cauterization to seal blood vessels, as well as the technique of

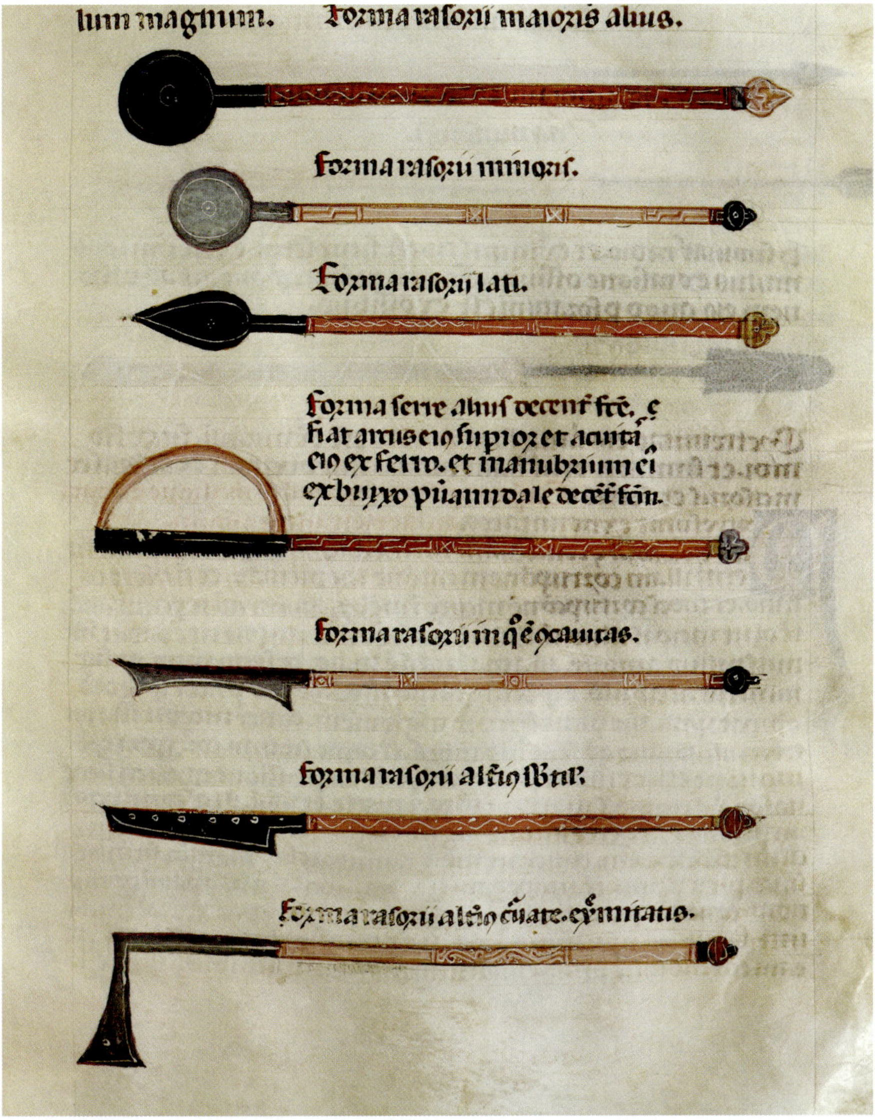

This page from a fourteenth-century Latin translation of *On Surgery* features diagrams of various surgical instruments available at the time of Albucasis's writing. Many of these instruments were developed b Albucasis, and some are even used today.

ligation, or tying off major blood vessels to prevent bleeding.

IMPORTANCE OF THE *AL-TASRIF*

More than just a technical manual, the *al-Tasrif* is a comprehensive set of recommendations for the practice of medicine. However, it was the first work in the Islamic world to treat surgery as a field of separate study distinct from the normal practice of medicine. Albucasis was very careful in his advice to those who wanted to become surgeons. He demanded that they take time to learn about the entire field of medicine before they attempted to specialize in one specific area and that they complete their studies of general medicine before they tried to perform surgery. This plan of learning is remarkably similar to our own modern system for training doctors, which requires that all physicians learn the basics of many disciplines before attempting to become specialists.

Just as Galen had codified the learning of antiquity and became the sole authority to which all physicians turned, so too did Albucasis codify all that had been learned since by Muslim physicians. His work was a great improvement on Galen's in many ways, for it included far more practical knowledge of human anatomy and was simply the greatest work on surgery ever written. In time it would displace Galen's work as the most influential medical text in Europe.

Galen and Albucasis were similar in another way as well: both lived during the height of their particular empire. However, the fall of Galen's Rome was several centuries away at the time of his death (and indeed, his part of the world would be ruled by its successor, the Byzantine Empire, for another thousand years). Albucasis was not so fortunate; within his lifetime he saw the collapse of the caliphate, invasion by foreigners and infidels, and the beginning of the end of the golden age of al-Andalus.

CHAPTER SIX

THE END OF MUSLIM POWER IN AL-ANDALUS

The *al-Tasrif* is recognized as one of the Middle Ages' most important works. Albucasis's scholarship was a monument to Islamic medicine. It was one of the last works of the caliphate of Córdoba, however. The glory of Medinat al-Zahra would soon be destroyed.

Al-Hakim II, the caliph who had employed Albucasis as his personal physician, died in 976. His nominal successor was his son, Hisham II, but power was actually in the hands of the ambitious vizier (prime minister) Abu Amir Muhammad ibn Abi Amir al-Maafari, who was given the title of Hajib al-Mansur ("the Victorious"; the title was Latinized to Almanzor, the name he is usually known in the West) because of his brilliant military campaigns against the Christian kingdoms of northern Iberia. While Hisham was kept occupied with the pleasures of his palace, al-Mansur ran the caliphate for him. His victories over the

Christians led to huge amounts of plundered wealth pouring into the coffers of Córdoba.

Although al-Mansur had brought untold riches and glory to the caliphate by his death in 1002, he had also exposed its weaknesses. It was possible for ambitious men to rise to great power and effectively control the government, and the wealth of al-Andalus would tempt many to attempt to do so.

BERBER REBELLION

Al-Mansur was briefly succeeded by his son, Abd al-Malik, but when he died prematurely in 1008, civil war broke out in the caliphate. A great-grandson of Abd al-Rahman III seized power from Hisham II and proclaimed himself the new caliph, Muhammad II. However, in North Africa, the Berber tribes themselves rebelled and proclaimed a different descendent of Abd al-Rahman, Suleiman, caliph. Soon a Berber army invaded Spain and marched on Córdoba, destroying Medinat al-Zahra in 1010. In a stunning reversal, Muhammad appealed to the Christians for help, and an army from Castile helped him defeat the Berbers in 1010. Muhammad was assassinated shortly after that, however, and Hisham II was returned to his throne.

Suleiman regrouped while his Berber armies terrorized the countryside. He besieged Córdoba until it surrendered in 1013. Although he would "rule" for three more years, for all intents and purposes the caliphate had been destroyed, although different men succeeded to the title until 1031. Al-Andalus fractured

Al-Mansur brought much wealth to the caliphate. He was known to plunder the Christian groups he conquered around northern Iberia, taking the prized possessions of their communities for possession by Córdoba.

completely under the strain of the civil war, breaking up into several small "states" commonly called the *taifa* (Arabic for "party" or "faction") kingdoms.

This presented the Christians with an opportunity they could not ignore. From the humble kingdom of Asturias, far to the north, had emerged several rapidly expanding kingdoms: Navarre, Aragon, and Castile, which were together rapidly becoming the most powerful unification in Spain. Under the leadership of her kings Ferdinand the Great, who held the throne from 1035–1065, and Alfonso the Brave, who ruled from

Even as the caliphate crumbled, unification among the Christian kingdoms was taking place. They took advantage of the states of al-Andalus, weakened by battle with the Berbers, and defeated the Moors in the Reconquest.

GERARD OF CREMONA

The Islamic world preserved many of the writings of the ancient Greeks that would have otherwise been lost. However, much of this work was translated into Arabic and thus was inaccessible to most scholars of Western Europe. One man, Gerard of Cremona, helped to start Europe's intellectual revolution by translating these works into Latin, the language of government, religion, and philosophy in Europe.

We know little about his life. He was born around 1114 in Cremona, a city in Lombardy (a region of northern Italy), where he became a scholar of philosophy. Finding that his Italian teachers did not have many ancient writings available to them—especially the great astronomer Ptolemy's *Almagest*—he decided to try and find copies of these works and translate them himself.

By 1144 Gerard was in Toledo, where he was able to learn Arabic and begin to work on the translations that would make him famous.

Gerard's translation of the *Almagest* was the only one available in Europe until the late fifteenth century, when Greek versions were discovered and translated into Latin. He translated Euclid's *Geometry* and many original works by Islamic scholars. He also translated medical works, including Albucasis's *al-Tasrif* and the Canons of Avicenna. (Some scholars attribute these translations to a later Gerard, Gerard of Sabbionetta).

Gerard of Cremona died in Toledo in 1187, having laid the foundation for much of the intellectual revolutions of the thirteenth and fourteenth centuries in Europe.

1072–1109, Castile led the attacks against the Moors called the Reconquest.

ALBUCASIS FINDS A NEW AUDIENCE

The *taifa* kingdoms were not up to the task of resisting the Christians, and Castile and Aragon expanded southward into al-Andalus. In 1085, Alfonso captured Toledo, the old Visigothic capital of Spain. And in 1144, Gerard of Cremona arrived there to translate as many Arabic works as he could, including Albucasis's *al-Tasrif*.

From Toledo, the *al-Tasrif* spread throughout Christian Europe, its fame slowly growing. The great French surgeon Guy de Chauliac, in his work *Chiurgia Magna* (*Great Surgery*, itself used as a medical text for over three hundred years), quoted Albucasis more than two hundred times. In 1471, the *al-Tasrif* was printed in Venice and quickly became a standard medical text. As late as the sixteenth century another great French surgeon, Jacques Dalechamps, was quoting the *al-Tasrif*. Albucasis had well earned his title of "the chief of all surgeons," as Pietro Argallata called him in the fifteenth century.

However, as the glory of Albucasis's work increased, that of al-Andalus declined. The fall of

This illustration is from Gerard of Cremona's twelfth-century Latin translation of the Greek physician Galen's *Treatise on Medicine*.

Toledo was merely one of the disastrous losses it suffered during the eleventh century; in fact, all of the conquests of the Christians would become permanent. As the Spanish kingdoms gained power, they extracted tribute from the weak *taifa* kingdoms, rich sums of gold that they used to further their military aims both in Spain and in the Mediterranean.

THE ALMORAVID CALIPHATE

These conquests attracted the attention of the rest of the Islamic world. In the 1050s a fundamentalist movement swept Morocco. Called the Almoravids in Spain (from the Arabic word *al-Murabit*, which means "a religious ascetic"), they practiced an especially strict form of Islam.

The continuing success of the Christians caused the leaders of the *taifa* kingdoms, with great reluctance, to invite the Almoravids into Spain to help them fight the Castilians. Their fears were justified; although the Almoravids halted the Christian advance, they soon turned on the *taifa* kingdoms, which they considered hopelessly corrupt, and by 1090, they had conquered them and reunified al-Andalus and North Africa.

The Almoravid caliphate was far stricter than the Umayyad caliphate had been. They rejected the rich lifestyles the caliphs of Córdoba had once enjoyed. They were also far less tolerant of Jews and Christians than the Umayyad caliphs had been.

However, within fifty years of ruling al-Andalus, the Almoravid caliphs were guilty of many of the same vices of which they had accused the Umayyads. Disunity followed: Arab against Berber, natives of Spain against the invading Almoravids; once again the Christians stepped up their attacks. And fundamentalist Berbers from North Africa's Almohad dynasty again rescued al-Andalus.

A PERIOD OF MORE UNREST

Almohad was a name taken from the Arabic *al-Muwahhidun* ("Monotheist" or "Unitarian"). Like the Almoravids before them, they were fanatics dedicated to the purification of Islam and the defeat of the infidel. They swept into Spain and defeated the Christians, holding them back for another century.

Almohad rule became gentler in time, and a second great period of art and literature eventually bloomed under their reign. This was the time that the great philosopher Averroes was living and writing in Spain.

The Christian kingdoms continued to gain power, however, and even the fresh blood the Almohads

Christian kingdoms increasingly gained power, until, with the marriage of Ferdinand and Isabella, they had defeated all of the Moor-ruled states in Spain.

brought to Spain could not stop their advance. In 1212, the emir Muhammad III al-Nasir was defeated by the combined forces of Castile, Aragon, Portugal, and Navarre at the battle of Las Navas de Tolosa. Within a decade all of Muslim Spain had been reclaimed by the Christians, except for the small state of Granada on the Mediterranean coast—and Granada paid a huge yearly tribute to the Spanish. In 1474, the marriage of Ferdinand of Aragon and Isabella of Castile united the two largest Spanish kingdoms; together, in 1491, they defeated Granada and ended the existence of the last Moorish state in Spain, one year before Columbus left for the New World.

For seven hundred years, an Islamic state existed on the European continent, in what would become the most powerful kingdom in western Europe during the sixteenth century. When the Moors invaded Spain, they brought with them the only living tradition of the ancient Mediterranean world. Their learning and culture far outstripped that of the barbarian princes they conquered, so much so that they disdained the pale infidels from over the Pyrenees and had as little to do with them as possible. As for the Europeans, they hated the brilliant people to the south and waged an unceasing war to oust them.

For a brief seven hundred years in al-Andalus a culture came into being that incorporated the best of three worlds: the Islamic world, the ancient Greek world, and the new world of Europe that was being born. It was an age of great wealth and great sophistication, of respect for the accumulated wisdom of the past and a thirst for even greater knowledge. During this short summer of knowledge and learning, men not only preserved the past but also helped light the way for the future, and in the field of medicine, perhaps no man did more than Albucasis.

GLOSSARY

Ali Muhammad's cousin and son-in-law, the fourth caliph, revered by Shia Muslims as the true successor to Muhammad. Ali was assassinated in 661, and his son Husayn was assassinated in 671 in Persia (present-day Karbala, Iraq), the act that made the division between Sunni and Shia permanent.

Allah The name of God in Arabic, the language of Muhammad and Islam. It means "God" or "The Only God."

Asia Minor The peninsula of Asia that juts out into the Aegean Sea that is presently occupied by Turkey.

Balkan Peninsula A mountainous peninsula in southern Europe, where Greece, Albania, Serbia, and Bulgaria are located today.

Berbers The nomadic people of North Africa. They were converted to Islam in the seventh century and formed the bulk of the Muslim armies that invaded Spain in 710.

Byzantine Empire The eastern half of the Roman Empire, which survived for one thousand years after the fall of Rome. It took its name from the original name of its capital city of Constantinople, Byzantium. It declined when the Islamic Turks finally captured Constantinople in 1453.

caliph The title given to the successors to Muhammad as the spiritual and temporal rulers of all Muslims. The Umayyad rulers of al-Andalus claimed the title in 929, although many Muslims dispute their right to it.

emir The Arabic word for an important noble who ruled a large region; it could mean "governor," but as these rulers were generally independent, it is probably best to translate it as "prince."

empirically Using observation and experiment as a method of making scientific discoveries.

Five Pillars The core beliefs of Islam, consisting of submission to Allah, prayer, fasting, charity, and pilgrimage to Mecca.

Galen The Greek-speaking Roman citizen whose systemization of Hippocrates's work would be the main medical technique in Europe and the Middle East for more than one thousand years.

Hellenization The spread of Greek culture, philosophy, and language.

heretic A person who doesn't believe in or who challenges a religion's doctrines.

Hippocrates The ancient Greek physician and healer who laid the foundations of modern medicine.

infidel Term used to describe a person who does not believe in or follow one's own religion.

Islam The name of the religion founded by Muhammad, known as the Prophet, in 610. The name means "submission (to God)."

Kaaba The large black cube-shaped shrine in Mecca, the holiest shrine in the Islamic world. Millions of pilgrims to Mecca visit it every year.

Mecca The city in central Arabia, the birthplace of Muhammad and the holiest place in the Islamic world; all Muslims are supposed to pray in its direction five times a day.

Moors The name given to the Berber peoples of North Africa by the Spanish.

mosque The house of worship for Muslims.

Muhammad The prophet who founded Islam. Born in Mecca, he lived from 571 CE to 632 CE.

Muslim A follower of Islam.

Persia An ancient empire in the Middle East, occupying the region now called Iraq.

Phoenicians An ancient sea-trading people who lived in what is now Syria and Lebanon. They introduced writing to the Greeks, and their descendents, the Carthaginians, ruled much of the Mediterranean and North Africa until the time of the Romans.

Quran The holy book of Islam, sometimes spelled Koran. It was dictated to the prophet Muhammad by the angel Gabriel.

Shia A large sect of Muslims that separated from the Sunnis after the assassination of Ali. Shia Muslims represent the majority in present-day Iraq and Iran.

Sunni The largest sect of Islam. Sunni Muslims reject the Shia claim that Ali was the rightful successor to

Muhammad. Most Arabic and African Muslims are Sunni.

Umayyad Dynasty of caliphs that ruled the Muslim world until 750. A lone survivor of the dynasty reached Spain, where his successors would rule until 1036.

Visigoths Germanic tribe that invaded the Roman Empire in the fifth century CE, eventually settling in Spain, where they ruled until being conquered by the Moors.

vizier Arabic title meaning prime minister; the most important official at the court of an emir.

FOR MORE INFORMATION

Arab Science and Technology Foundation
P.O. Box 2668
Sharjah, United Arab Emirates
+ 971 6 5584330
Website: http://www.astf.net/
The Arab Science and Technology Foundation is an independent, non-profit, non-governmental organization that works regionally and internationally to encourage investment in science and technology.

International Society for the History of Islamic Medicine (ISHIM)
P.O. Box 239
Manama
Kingdom of Bahrain
Website: http://www.ishim.net
The mission of ISHIM is to promote public awareness of the contributions of Arab and Muslim physicians to the history of medicine. The organization achieves through encouraging more research and academic studies of earlier Islamic medicine, public outreach, and the establishment of a museum.

Islamic Educational, Scientific, and Cultural Organization (ISESCO)
Avenue des F.A.R, Hay Ryad
P.O. Box 2275
+ 212 (0) 5 37 56 60 52 / 53
PC Code 10104 - Rabat - Kingdom of Morocco
Website: http://www.isesco.org.ma
(ISESCO) promotes cultural engagement and coordination in education, science, culture, and communication to highlight the achievements of Islamic culture and support socio-cultural development. The organization works closely with a number of international organizations on dialogue projects, especially the United Nations.

Metropolitan Museum of Modern Art
1000 Fifth Avenue
New York, NY 10028
(212) 535-7710
Website: http://www.metmuseum.org/
The Metropolitan Museum of Modern Art features a collection of artifacts related to astronomy and astrology in the medieval Islamic world.

Museum of Science and Technology in Islam
4700 King Abdullah University of Science & Technology
Thuwal, Jeddah 23955-6900
Kingdom of Saudi Arabia
Website: http://museum.kaust.edu.sa/

This museum is part of King Abdullah University of Science and Technology. It explores Islamic contributions to science and technology.

WEBSITES

Because of the changing nature of Internet links, Rosen Publishing has developed an online list of websites related to the subject of this book. This site is updated regularly. Please use this link to access the list:

http://www.rosenlinks.com/PSMI/albuca

FOR FURTHER READING

Al-Khalili, Jim. *The House of Wisdom: How Arabic Science Saved Ancient Knowledge and Gave Us the Renaissance*. New York: Penguin Press, 2011.

Al-Khalili, Jim. *Pathfinders: The Golden Age of Arabic Science*. London: Penguin, 2012.

Barber, Nicola. *Medieval Medicine*. Chicago, IL: Raintree, 2013.

Belting, Hans. *Florence and Baghdad: Renaissance Art and Arab Science*. Cambridge, MA: Belknap Press of Harvard University Press, 2011.

Bobrick, Benson. *The Caliph's Splendor: Islam and the West in the Golden Age of Baghdad*. New York: Simon & Schuster, 2012.

Clarke, Nicola. *The Muslim Conquest of Iberia: Medieval Arabic Narratives*. New York: Routledge, 2012.

Collins, Roger. *Caliphs and Kings: Spain, 796-1031*. Malden, MA: Wiley-Blackwell, 2012.

Fuess, Albrecht, and Jan-Peter Hartung. *Court Cultures in the Muslim World: Seventh to Nineteenth Centuries*. New York: Routledge, 2011.

Hitchcock, Richard. *Muslim Spain Reconsidered: From 711 to 1502*. Edinburgh, Scotland: Edinburgh University Press, 2014.

Jackson, Mark. *The Oxford Handbook of the History of Medicine*. Oxford, England: Oxford University Press, 2011.

Lapidus, Ira M. *A History of Islamic Societies*. New York: Cambridge University Press, 2014.

Nardo, Don. *The Birth of Islam*. Greensboro, NC: Morgan Reynolds Publishing, 2012.

Roscoe, Kelly, and Mick Isle. *Aristotle: The Father of Logic*. New York: Rosen Publishing, 2016.

Ruthven, Malise. *Islam: A Very Short Introduction*. New York: Oxford University Press, 2012.

Scherer, Lauri S. *Islam*. Detroit, MI: Greenhaven Press, 2012.

Sharaf al-Din, Fatimah, and Intilaq Muhammad Ali. *The Amazing Discoveries of Ibn Sina*. Toronto, Ontario: Groundwood Books, 2015.

York, William Henry. *Health and Wellness in Antiquity Through the Middle Ages*. Santa Barbara, CA: Greenwood, 2012.

BIBLIOGRAPHY

Fletcher, Richard. *Moorish Spain*. Berkeley, CA: University of California Press, 1993.

Lane-Poole, Stanley. *The Story of the Moors in Spain*. Baltimore, MD: Black Classic Press, 1990.

Nasr, Seyyed Hossein. *Science and Civilization in Islam*. Cambridge, MA: Harvard University Press, 1968.

Porter, Roy. *The Greatest Benefit to Mankind: A Medical History of Humanity*. New York: W. W. Norton & Company, 1997.

Siraisi, Nancy G. *Medieval and Early Renaissance Medicine*. Chicago: The University of Chicago Press, 1990.

Watt, W. Montgomery. *The Majesty That Was Islam*. New York: Praeger Publishers, 1974.

INDEX

A

Abd-ar-Rahman, 41, 74, 87
Alexander the Great, 12, 15, 16, 54, 55, 63, 64
Alfonso the Brave, 90, 92
Almoravid caliphate, 94–95
anatomy, 7, 46, 48, 54–55, 59, 81, 84–85
Andalus, al-, 6–7, 41, 42, 44–45, 74, 85, 87, 88, 92, 95, 98
  philosophers of, 67, 69
Aristotle, 6, 10, 12, 54, 58, 70, 72, 77
Asclepiadae, 48, 49
Asia Minor, 9, 12, 55
Averroes, 70–71, 95
Avicenna, 75, 91
  contributions to medicine, 69, 72

B

Baghdad, 8, 27, 41, 42
Bedouins, 16–17
Berbers, 35, 95
  rebellion of, 87–88, 90, 92
Byzantine Empire, 6, 24, 33, 63, 64, 85
  and the Bedouins, 16–17

C

caliphate of Córdoba, 42, 44, 85, 86, 87, 88, 94–95
caliphs, 27, 35, 39, 41, 61, 66, 74, 86, 87
Carthage, 29–30
Christianity, 22, 27, 30–31, 34, 39, 44, 58–59, 75, 82, 83, 86–87, 89, 92, 94, 95, 97
Córdoba, 7, 27, 41, 86–87, 88
  Albucasis in, 42, 44–45
  caliphate of, 74, 86, 94–95

D

Damascus, 39, 41
diseases, 6, 46, 48, 49, 51, 54, 58, 59, 60, 66, 69, 72, 77
  hereditary, 82, 84
Doubts About Galen, 67, 69

E

Egypt, 9, 12, 15, 24, 26, 46, 48–49, 55
emirs, 39, 70, 95, 97

F

Five Pillars of Islam, 20–21
France, 6–7, 33–34, 39, 42

G

Galen, 67, 69, 71, 84–85
building on Hippocrates, 55–56, 58–59, 60
Gerard of Cremona, 91, 92
Greeks, 6, 10, 12, 17, 27, 29, 30, 45, 52, 54–55, 70, 91, 98
culture of, 12, 15–16
knowledge, 63–64
medicine of, 48–49, 55
philosophers, 58, 61, 67
physicians, 67, 69, 80

H

Hakim, al-, II, 45, 74, 86
Hippocrates, 49, 51, 52, 54, 77
Galen building upon the work of, 55–56, 58–59, 60
Hippocratic oath, 52–53
Hisham II, 86, 87

I

Iberian Peninsula, 6–7, 29, 30, 36, 39
Ibn Zayid, Tariq, 35–36
India, 12, 17, 26, 64, 66
infidels, 85, 95, 98
Islam
creation of, 17
emergence of in Arabia, 29
revelation of, 18, 22–23, 24, 26
spread into North Africa, 35
Italy, 16, 29, 33, 91

M

Macedonia, 12, 15, 16, 64
Mansur, al-, 86, 87
mathematics, 7, 9, 46, 66
Mecca, 18, 20, 21, 22, 23, 24
medicine, 6, 46, 63–64, 66, 67, 69, 74, 77, 80, 82, 84, 86, 98
Albucasis's method of practicing, 74–75, 76
Avicenna's contributions to, 69, 72
Greek, 48, 49, 54, 55, 56, 60
Mesopotamia, 8–10, 24, 26, 48, 64
Moors, 35, 36, 38, 39, 41, 90, 92, 98

P

Persians, 9, 10, 12, 15, 17, 24, 66
Prophet (Muhammad), 8, 20, 27, 35, 39, 60, 63
  and the revelation of Islam, 18, 22–23, 24, 26

Q

Quran, 18, 22, 72

R

Rhazes, 67, 69, 72
Rodrigo, 35, 38
  opponents of, 35–36
Roman Empire, 6, 7, 15, 24, 27, 29, 30–31, 33, 34, 35, 45, 54, 60, 61, 64
  eastern half of, 16–17
  imperial system of, 31, 33
  rise and fall of, 15–16

S

Shia Muslims, 21, 39, 66
Spain, 6–7, 27, 61, 87, 92, 94, 95, 97
  Arabs and Moors in, 35, 98
  conquered by the Visigoths, 33–34, 36
  early history of, 29–31
  Muslim conquest of, 36, 39, 41, 44
  unification of, 88, 90, 97
Sunni Muslims, 21, 39, 66
surgery, 6, 7, 46, 74, 75, 77, 78, 80–82, 84–85
Syria, 17, 18, 24, 39, 63

T

Tasrif, al-, 7, 75, 77, 80, 82, 86, 91, 92
  importance of, 84–85

U

Umayyad caliphate, 36, 39, 41, 94, 95

V

Visigoths, 31, 33–34, 36, 38, 92

ABOUT THE AUTHORS

Bridget Lim has taught history and religion at the high school level. Currently, she is pursuing a PhD in Islamic Studies.

Fred Ramen is a writer and computer programmer who lives in New York City with his wife, Allison. He is the author of fifteen books for Rosen Publishing on subjects ranging from Jerry West to tuberculosis. In 1997 he was a five-time undefeated champion on the television show Jeopardy!

PHOTO CREDITS

Cover Sheila Terry/Science Source; cover (background), pp. 3, 20, 21, 38, 52, 53, 70, 71, 91 gfxmart/Shutterstock.com; p. 5 Iqbal Khatri/Moment/Getty Images; pp. 6-7 kickimages/E+/Getty Images; pp. 10-11 Dorling Kindersley/Getty Images; pp. 13, 32-33 Print Collector/Hulton Archive/Getty Images; pp. 14-15 Peter Hermes Furian/Shutterstock.com; pp. 18-19 Werner Forman/Universal Images Group/ Getty Images; pp. 24-25 Pictures from History/Bridgeman Images; p. 28 Private Collection/© Bianchetti/Leemage/Bridgeman Images; pp. 36-37 Universal Images Group/Getty Images; p. 40 Private Collection/Bridgeman Images; pp. 42-43 Artur Bogacki/Shutterstock.com; p. 47 Science Museum, London, Wellcome Images; p. 50 British Library, London, UK/ © British Library Board. All Rights Reserved/Bridgeman Images; pp. 56-57 Private Collection/© Look and Learn/ Bridgeman Images; pp. 62-63 Culture Club/Hulton Archive/Getty Images; pp. 64-65 Bibliotheque Nationale, Paris, France/Archives Charmet/Bridgeman Images; p.68 Wellcome Library, London; p. 73 Scala/White Images/Art Resource, NY; p. 76 DEA/G. Dagli Orti/De Agostini/Getty Images; p. 79 Buyenlarge/Archive Photos/ Getty Images; p. 83 DEA/M. Seemuller/De Agostini/Getty Images; pp. 88-89 British Library, London, UK/Bridgeman Images; p. 90 Photo © Tarker/Bridgeman Images; p. 93 Iberfoto/SuperStock; pp. 96-97 MPI/Hulton Royals Collection/Getty Images; additional cover and interior background patterns and textures javarman/ Shutterstock.com, Dragana Jokmanovic/Shutterstock.com; back cover pattern MaryMo/Shutterstock.com

Designer: Michael Moy; Editor: Christine Poolos;
Photo Researcher: Nicole DiMella